after they've gone
their blessings continue

Deborah Nelles

illustrations & reflection questions by Linda McCray
foreword by Carol B. Donnelly

A Flock of Doves Publishing, LLC

I hope this book can help in any healing in your life.

© 2014 by Deborah Nelles

Illustrations, reflection questions and graphic design by Linda McCray

All rights reserved. No portion of this book may be reproduced in any form, including electronic, without the written permission of the publisher except for brief excerpts used in media reviews.

ISBN: 978-1-4951-3242-1

Published by A Flock of Doves Publishing, LLC
AFlockOfDoves.com

Printed in United States of America

Dedication

To my parents, Max and Virg.

Acknowledgments

The 31 after-death communications you have sent to me over these past years provide the basis for this book. Not only have your communications, my visible blessings, both intrigued and delighted me, but also on a deeper level, they have strengthened and comforted me. Most importantly, they have let me know you continue to watch over me, that I am not alone.

To Mike, my husband, your continual encouragement, support, humor and love keep me strong and moving forward. As you say, "it's all good."

To Joanne, who has so faithfully worked with me on every word and every page of this book, your suggestions and insights have been invaluable. Your determination and heart led to the discovery of truly amazing quotes that reflect the essence of the book. We did it.

Linda, your enthusiasm from the very beginning has made this book a beautiful thing. Your artistic creativity and mastery has made this book come alive.

Barbara, while you were last to join this group, I've learned to rely on your knowledge and expertise.

I couldn't have a better team and I truly thank you all.

To all of the people who heard the idea in the beginning and encouraged and supported me in its development, I thank you.

Table of Contents

Foreword 7
In the Beginning 9
Sender — Virgil 13
Sender — Maxine 15

Visible Blessings

Trapper 18
Dad and the Rosebush 23
The Piano 27
The Gift 31
Three Fishermen in Streams 35
Woman in the Stream 39
Squirrels and Magpies 42
The Garden Squirrel 47
It's a Wonderful World 51
Mother Bombie 55
Pennies 59
Damien and Max 62
The Pass 67
Dime — CD Player 71
Shadrach, Meshach, and Abednego 75
Gibson Park 79
Don Juan 83
Wandering Woman 87
Angel on the Tree 90
Chickadees on the Rail 95
The Vase 99
Monarch Butterfly 103
Dove on the Rail 107
Solitaire 111
Mother as a Young Girl 115
Milkshake 119
Cricket Outside 123
Doves, Salt Lake City 127
Sirius Radio 131
Oprah 134
"Ragtime Cowboy Joe" 139

Afterword 142

Foreword

There is a term "no-moreness" that aptly describes the grief with the loss of a loved one. The absence of that person in our lives is the deepest sorrow, and we long to be assured that somehow he or she remains with us. Sometimes memories keep our loved one present to us. But occasionally it seems that a contact is more than a memory.

The line between this world and the other is a thin one. When a close relationship has formed between people, it would seem that death does not abruptly end this relationship.

I had the pleasure of knowing Virgil and Maxine Nelles for many years, both when I lived in Montana and later when I visited. As we camped and fished in the Montana wilderness, I learned not only to love nature, but to love and respect Virgil and Maxine. Often their daughter Deborah would be along on these excursions. As a teenager, her relationship with her parents was typically complex. As she moved into adulthood, the love that they shared was evident, even as she chose paths that were incompatible with the values of her parents. There always remained a steadfast love and support and caring for each other. As time went on, Deb and I became good friends.

The deaths of her parents, first Virgil and then Maxine, were deeply traumatic experiences for Deb. She was both surprised and awed when she began to be aware of ways in which her parents continued to communicate with her. Because she was open to this communication, it was a great comfort to her. Before long Deborah began to hear from other people who had received messages or favors from loved ones who had died. Her book is based primarily on her own experiences, and she hopes that it will give relevance to all who have maintained some closeness to those who have moved to the next world.

"Death does not extinguish light. It puts out the lamp because the dawn has come."* It is perhaps, in this dawn, that hands touch from one world to another. For all of us who have received this blessing, it is the greatest gift of love.

Carol B. Donnelly, LCSW, Jungian Analyst
Retired

*Rabindranath Tagore

In the Beginning
February 14, 2005

It was February 14, 2005, Valentine's Day. My cousin Vicky called to tell me my 92-year-old mother, in the hospital, was not doing well and I needed to come home. Mother lived two hours away, a nice drive in summer, but it was winter now and we were in the middle of a snowstorm and I feared the drive ahead.

The weather felt as overwhelming as my mood. I had dreaded this day for so long, feeling so unprepared to face this possible transition. I called my husband, Mike, to let him know what was happening. I pulled on my boots and coat, got in the car. "Drive, drive, drive," I thought.

I don't remember the time passing, yet soon I was pulling into the hospital parking lot. I found my mother's room, greeted my cousin, and went to my mother. She was gaunt, frail and her face had red blotches caused by the medicine. I held her hand, fearing a hug might have caused her discomfort.

"Mom," I said, "I need to talk to you." She looked closely into my eyes. "If you're going to pass soon, I want you to promise you will send me a sign to let me know you are okay." She didn't skip a beat as she replied, "I'm not sure I know how." She turned to my cousin who said, "You'll know at the time, Max."

We all quieted and felt content with that answer. Over the next fifteen days my mother's health continually rose and fell, as did our hearts and hopes. When my mother said, "I know you're all waiting for me to pass, but I'm not ready to go yet," the other family members returned to their homes. That was that.

She was transferred to another care facility. The last night I spoke with her she was planning on having her hair "permed" the next day. She passed away the next morning at 10:10 A.M.

People of all cultures and faiths hold disparate views of what happens when the body ceases to function. Is death the end? Is it a transition to another realm? Is there a heaven? Is there a hell? This book will not attempt to answer any of those questions. It is not a scientific inquiry into such matters.

My book is a compilation of communications, primarily from my mother, but some from my father, which have come to me since their deaths. My parents never communicated through dreams, but have somehow found a slit between realities which lets them send me tailor-made messages. My role in the process has been to stay open, stay awake. I have been greatly comforted and remain in awe.

I hope my readers will be intrigued by these visible blessings. I would like to introduce you to my parents, Virgil and Maxine, the senders.

For all that has been? Thanks!
For all that will be? Yes!

Dag Hammarskjöld

Journal entries by Hammarskjöld, published in 1964
Excerpts from *Markings*

Sender - Virgil

Dad meets new friend out camping.

My father, Virgil, was born in Minnesota in a small farming community. Like his parents he was Roman Catholic, a faith that sustained him all of his life. In many ways my father was a contradiction. He was quick to anger yet just as quick to laugh. He left home shortly after high school to move to Montana where he remained until his death at eighty-two.

Dad absolutely adored my mother and, while he loved us kids, I don't think he knew what to do with us once we became older with individual personalities and temperaments of our own, especially if that included rebelliousness on our part.

When Dad was forty years old he was diagnosed with multiple sclerosis, a disease that would eventually disable him and place him in a nursing home. But up until that time my parents had a wonderful life, camping and fishing, trailering and traveling.

My dad particularly loved the home they had built when they were first married. Like his parents, he had gardening/farming in his genes and he spent hours landscaping our yard, with our dog always by his side. He especially loved tending to his magnificent Floribunda rose bushes. We always had a small vegetable garden and food for the birds and squirrels.

As Dad aged he was somehow able to find acceptance of his many losses: his home, his health, his vision, his mobility. And yet, before my eyes, I saw this man grow into himself. We never had a deep philosophical discussion and yet in our moments of silence we shared everything.

> ***Nowhere can a man find a quieter
> or more untroubled retreat
> than in his own soul.***
>
> Marcus Aurelius
>
> *Meditations*
> Book 4, Section 5

Sender - Maxine

Mother was redheaded, and fire was her astrological element. I think she always wanted to be the type of person who colored within the lines, and yet her incredibly vibrant spirit kept her reaching, learning, growing in unique and somewhat unconventional ways. Like my father she was Roman Catholic. Hers was a lived faith both strong and dynamic.

Mother doing what she loved best.

By the age of fourteen she was proficient enough on the piano that she was able to accompany her older brother when he played saxophone at the local speakeasies. Of course my grandmother was along for these performances, standing guard. Montana in those days could be a pretty rugged place.

After graduating from high school Mother entered the University of Montana as a pharmacy student. Although medicine had been her preferred choice of study, her father was adamantly opposed to this, and sadly, that was that. And so mother entered the pharmacy program, one of only three women in her class. She earned her diploma and entered into a pharmacy practice.

She then met my father, something having to do with a golf game, although I was never clear on the details. They married and settled into their home. Their first major purchase was my mother's piano, a Baldwin Acrosonic, Mother's joy.

Mother's second great passion had to do with her love of the outdoors. Whether camping in a tent or a trailer, Mother's ideal day would begin early in the morning. She would pull on her hip boots and waders, place the fly rod in her hand and then head out for one of her favorite fishing holes. She always returned with a "mess" of fish.

The day was not complete, however, until the campfire was lit and

Mother's strong alto voice led us in song. Of course, we were missing the piano for the full effect. Mother, not to be deterred, pulled out her baritone ukulele and we sang in harmony until the stars came out.

My relationship with Mother was often a difficult one. As I stretched my wings to fly higher, she saw not the grandeur of my vision, but only my erratic dips and dives. This scared her, but angered her even more, as she realized she had no ability to call me back.

Once I had obtained my education and quieted my wanderlust I returned home and Mother and I began to gingerly rebuild our relationship. We discussed, we shared, we argued, we laughed, and then we did it all over again. Above all we grew, sometimes in lopsided ways, eventually discovering our harmony.

***I want to go on living
even after death!***

Anne Frank

The Diary of a Young Girl,
also known as the Diary of Anne Frank

Visible Blessing - Trapper
January 17, 1992

I had just relocated to Cheney, Washington, to attend graduate school. Although I had a master's degree in sociology, I realized I needed a second master's in social work to strengthen and expand my mental health counseling practice.

I rented the downstairs of a home located outside of town on several acres. I had been in school for three months when I got a phone call from my mother, saying my father was ill and not expected to survive. By this time, it was winter and as I set out for the long drive home I didn't feel the usual apprehension, knowing I had two passes to cross and potentially icy roads. As I recall, the roads were bare, and even if they weren't I drove as though they were.

When I entered my father's room he had just slipped into a coma, and I would never again see him in life. We set up a vigil in his room and waited for other family members to arrive. We each said goodbye to our father and he slipped from life.

After the funeral I returned to school and attempted to reorder my forever altered life. As I reflected on my relationship with my father, I realized we had gone through many phases. We were extremely close when I was young, conflicted intensely during my teens and twenties, but we had begun to build a stronger yet still tentative relationship lately. I also realized that while it was one thing to know I could always call Dad every few days or weeks, that option was gone forever now.
I knew I would never hear him say, "Well good morning, Honey, so good of you to call."

As he aged and was tempered by life, he had become so gracious and so kind, yet he always retained his mischievous sense of humor.
As I healed I found solace in talking to Dad outside, in the backyard under the stars. On these nights, we talked as we never had in life.

When I came to Cheney I had brought two dogs with me, Gretel, a miniature schnauzer and Cassie, a mixed breed. Both were sweet and I loved them, but neither provided the companionship I now needed.

I considered getting another dog, but felt the time wasn't right. I settled in and let life soften the tender places in my heart.

One day when I returned home and pulled into the gravel driveway, there stood a beautiful black and white dog. He looked like a border collie cross. He appeared healthy and well loved, yet seemed a little shy.

"Someone surely must be looking for you," I thought. I put an ad in the paper, and checked local fliers to see if I could locate his people. In the weeks that followed, no one responded to my queries. I put a collar on him, named him Trapper, and called him mine.

As I thought about this most wonderful gift, I saw the hand and heart of my father. After all, hadn't my father and I spent a lifetime loving and caring for our pups?!

Now when the morning sun was up, I would put on my hiking clothes, call to Gretel, Cassie and the ever exuberant Trapper, and off we went, heading into the hills.

"Hurry, hurry," called Trapper. "So very much to see and do." As we walked, I could feel my father beside us, eyes sparkling and a playful smile on his face.

But I know, somehow,
that only when it is dark enough,
can you see the stars.

Martin Luther King, Jr.

Speech delivered at Bishop Charles Temple
in Memphis, Tennessee
April 3, 1968

I saw the hand and heart of my father

My Journal

What was your relationship like with your loved one that has gone before you? What gifts have you received that reminds your heart of them?

Visible Blessing - Dad and the Rosebush
June 25, 1992

When I remember my childhood home, the scene that comes to mind is my father in the backyard tending to his beloved rose garden. I never knew what magic elixir my father put on the rose bushes, but the roses thrived year in, year out. When my parents were forced to sell their home, my father went into a nursing home and my mother moved into an apartment.

As a housewarming gift, I bought Mother a small pink rosebush, thinking it would make her apartment more festive. I teasingly called her "Black Thumb" because she had no aptitude for nurturing plants, and like the young child who promises to take care of the new puppy, I told Mother I would tend the rosebush.

My father died December 13, Friday the 13th. That spring, when I was over at Mother's, I glanced at the sadly neglected rosebush and noticed it was growing. Feeling guilty for promises unkept, I spruced up the rosebush.

"Not bad," I thought. Each week when I went to Mother's, to my surprise I saw that the rose bush had grown. I began calling the rosebush Mother's "Jack and the Beanstalk" rosebush. And then the blossoms came. They were stunning. Big, bold, and beautiful. When friends would come by they would look at the rosebush and simply say, "I see your father's been busy."

"Yes," I thought, "he has."

"Take me into the garden, my boy," he said at last. "And tell me all about it." And so they led him in.

The place was a wilderness of autumn gold and purple and violet blue and flaming scarlet and on every side were sheaves of late lilies standing together—lilies which were white or white and ruby. He remembered well when the first of them had been planted that just at this season of the year their late glories should reveal themselves. Late roses climbed and hung and clustered and the sunshine deepening the hue of the yellowing trees made one feel that one stood in an embowered temple of gold. The newcomer stood silent just as the children had done when they came into its grayness. He looked round and round.

"I thought it would be dead," he said.

"Mary thought so at first," said Colin. "But it came alive."

Frances Hodgson Burnett

"In the Garden"
The Secret Garden

Your father's been busy

My Journal

How has a special moment with your loved one touched your life? What has blossomed from it?

Visible Blessing - The Piano
March 3, 2005

It was March 3, 2005. Since I had spoken with my mother the night before and she seemed to be doing well I answered the phone without concern. It was my cousin, however, letting me know Mother had died.

I lost my breath, and try as I might to deny the passage, I knew it was true. I was torn open. I sat on the floor not knowing what to do. My tears flowed freely. When I looked inside myself I found a helpless and frightened child, standing alone.

Around two hours later, the time it took to travel from Mother's bedside to my home, there was a knock on the door. I didn't want to see or talk to anyone, but the knocking was insistent. I forced myself to open the door. There stood the movers with Mother's piano. I knew it would be coming at some point after her death, but it took Mother's passage to release it. I felt comforted and thought, "How perfect." Mother had sent her last gift to me, her piano.

I was born around the same year my parents bought the piano. To us, it was a living presence, a member of the family. Rarely would a day go by without Mother sitting down to play the piano, whether for five minutes or fifty minutes. How often my night dreams were wrapped in Mother's piano song.

Now the piano was in my home. It didn't feel right. I think the piano also felt forlorn, knowing no other hands could bring it to life, could coax magic from its keys as Mother had.

I sat on the piano bench hearing the music of my lifetime. I closed my eyes and saw Mother's strong and capable hands dancing across the keys.

And then I realized Mother had been true to her word that day in the hospital when she promised I would hear from her. Her visible blessings had begun.

*All the darkness in the world
cannot extinguish the light of a single candle.*

Source Unknown, Attributed to St. Francis of Assisi

Her visible blessings had begun.

My Journal

What visible or invisible blessings
have you received through your tears?

Visible Blessing – The Gift
March 4, 2005

Mother was 85 when she realized she could no longer live on her own and needed to move into a retirement community. Although she would be on the independent-living side of the facility, the move represented a further letting go of those things that had defined her life.

When Mother moved into the facility, she noticed that many residents had something distinctive on their entrance door, a wreath, pictures, something saying, "This is a part of who I am."

Mother thought a great deal about what would best represent her life and chose nature as her life theme. She went to a local design center where they created a nature sculpture. The sculpture had several tan, chocolate and rust branches and vines of various thicknesses in a large bronze pot. Throughout the sculpture were several small chickadees, one of Mother's favorite birds. The nature sculpture was both elegant and simple.

Mother stayed in independent living for seven years. Eventually her failing health caused her to move into assisted living. She could no longer keep the nature sculpture, and so it came to my home.

Mother only spent one day in the assisted living facility, then she experienced a major health crisis and went into the hospital. She died fifteen days later.

After Mother's passing, my friends and work colleagues contacted the local florist and had an arrangement sent to me. I broke into a smile when I saw it. Here in miniature was Mother's nature sculpture, a dark pot of tan, chocolate and rust intertwining vines, wrapped around a vibrant green plant and topped with miniature chickadees.

It has been nine years since Mother's passing. Her nature sculpture still sits on our porch by the front door. Periodically we go into the woods to replenish it with new branches and vines. The miniature sculpture Mother and my friends sent us is still healthy and vibrant in our kitchen.

I died as a mineral and became a plant,
I died as plant and rose to animal,
I died as animal and I was Man.
Why should I fear?
When was I less by dying?

Jalal al-Din Muhammad Rumi

as translated in *The Mystics of Islam* (1914),
edited by Reynold Alleyne Nicholson, p. 125

"This is a part of who I am."

My Journal

How is your loved one a part of who you are?
What represents their life?

Visible Blessing – Three Fishermen in Streams
May 7, May 20, June 3, 2005

It had been two months since Mother had died and I was feeling quite raw, trying to negotiate the unfamiliar land of grief. The daily emotional unevenness would take my breath away, bringing me peace at one moment, slamming me into despair at the next.

Mike and I decided to go to dinner at a local restaurant, thinking pizza sounded good. As we sat down to consider our order, I looked up and there on the back wall of the restaurant was a very large, very beautiful picture of a man fishing in a stream. The scene looked very familiar to me, having been in similar locations with Mother through the years. I found the picture and the associated emotions very comforting.

A few weeks later I had a doctor's appointment and I was somewhat uncomfortable as the doctor was new. I checked in, filled out the required paperwork and waited. When I was finally shown into the doctor's office, there was another picture of a fisherman in a stream. Although it was a different location, I felt the same emotional comfort.

Two weeks later I went into a clothing store. Although the store was quite different from either the pizza parlor or the doctor's office, there was another picture of a man fishing in a stream. It's hard to describe the feelings that I had when I saw this third picture. I felt as though Mother was with me still and for that moment the emotional upheavals I had been experiencing were quieted.

***The Miracles of the Church
seem to me not to rest so much upon faces
or voices or healing power
coming suddenly near to us from afar off,
but upon our perceptions being made finer,
so that for a moment our eyes can see
and our ears can hear
what is there about us always.***

Willa Cather

Death Comes for the Archbishop

The scene looked very familiar

My Journal

What pictures comfort you?

Visible Blessing – Woman in the Stream
July 25, 2005

It was 7:00 A.M. and I was heading to my outreach office two hours away. It was a wonderful day, warm and sunny, and I was looking forward to the drive. As I started out, I told Mother I hadn't heard from her in a while and hoped she would contact me.

I came to an area where the stream was flowing close by. To my amazement, there in the middle of the stream stood a woman fishing, rod in hand, dressed in hip boots and waders. Everything moved in slow motion. I looked left to see if there was a car, but there was none. I continued to stare, not believing my eyes. In more than fifteen years and hundreds of trips by this area, I had never seen anyone fishing here, much less a woman.

It's hard to describe what happens when an incident like this occurs. The logical side of my brain said, "Oh, a woman fishing in the stream, no big deal." The intuitive side of my brain was in awe. After I returned home a few days later, I tried to find a photo or painting of a woman fishing in a stream, but after looking at hundreds I discovered mostly men.

I finally contacted a friend of mine who is a professional artist and commissioned her to do a portrait of Mother fishing. When the painting was finished, it was all I had hoped it would be. And now, throughout the house, I can look at the paintings and photos of Mother, fishing rod in hand, casting her line into a rippling stream.

*Crazy Horse dreamed
and went into the world
where there is nothing
but the spirits of all things.
That is the real world
that is behind this one,
and everything we see
here is something like
a shadow from that one.*

Nicholas Black Elk

*Black Elk Speaks: Being the Life Story
of a Holy Man of the Oglala Sioux*

Casting her Line into a Rippling Stream

My Journal

Create a portrait, with word or image, of your loved one.

Visible Blessing – Squirrels and Magpies
June 6, 2005

My parents loved trailering or trailer camping and would often spend weeks at a time in some of their favorite spots.

On one of their outings there was a particularly friendly squirrel in camp.

Dad got a box of crackers and slowly enticed the squirrel onto his knee. He was delighted by the interaction, although the squirrel nails were quite sharp!

After Dad passed, I began to notice unusual squirrel appearances. One of my favorites happened a few years later. I was returning home from an overnight at a friend's. It was a lovely day. The temperature was perfect, with a bright blue sky. I wanted to get an early start, so I left around 7:00 a.m.

My friend lives on a hill. I drove down the first block. Out popped a squirrel running lickety-split across the road, right in front of my car. Luckily, I was paying attention and going slow, so the squirrel made it safely across the street.

I started down the second block and another squirrel made a wide arc in the road, returning to the sidewalk. I was wide awake by this time and starting to think this might be my dad saying good morning.

I started down the third block. Here came another squirrel. It also did a little dance in the road. "Good morning to you, too," I said, pretty sure by now it was my dad. I had a big grin on my face. What a lovely way to begin the day.

I am very aware that many people live in communities with large squirrel populations. I felt this incident was significant because for five years I had operated a satellite office and had rented a room from my friend, staying there one or two days every other week. I calculated that during the time I stayed there I traveled up and down a very busy and well travelled road over 222 times and, in all that time, I had not once seen a squirrel. And so, when three squirrels dramatically appeared in front of me three blocks in a row, it felt like communication from my father.

I went to my favorite drive-through coffee shop, bought my usual blueberry muffin and latte and turned towards the highway. As I came around the corner in the middle of the road there was a group of five or six magpies. There was no carrion in the road to attract their attention. Actually, they looked like they were having a morning meeting.

I drove my car forward slowly to get their attention but they were not interested and continued to congregate in the middle of the road. There was nothing I could do, so I put the car in park and waited to see what would happen next. After a few more minutes the magpies flew off and I headed towards home. I didn't know the import of the incident, but I felt it was significant.

When I arrived home I looked at the symbolism of the magpie. The Cheyenne believe the magpie is a secret messenger from the creator. The Chinese believe the magpie brings joy and good fortune.

What an incredible way to start the day!

*The universe is wider
than our views of it.*

Henry David Thoreau

Chapter 18: Conclusion
Walden; or, Life in the Woods.

It was a lovely day.

My Journal

What fond memories do you have of a lovely day with your loved one?

Visible Blessing - The Garden Squirrel
July 10, 2005

Like my father, I am also a gardener. At the first sign of spring, my garden gloves are on and I can be found early in the morning surrounded by my garden companions, the birds, squirrels, ladybugs, even the daddy longlegs.

Morning feels like sacred time as I begin to slowly clear away the weeds to showcase the lovely flowers that are beginning to bud.

One morning when I was totally absorbed in the garden cleaning process, I looked up, and three feet away was a large older squirrel. My first feeling was fear that it might be rabid. I had never before had a squirrel sit so close, seemingly undeterred by my presence. As time went by, the squirrel and I shared a companionable space. My thoughts, of course, turned to my father who had similarly spent hours early in the mornings in his garden.

As I was working I looked closely into the eyes of the squirrel and as odd as it may seem, I saw and felt a connection with my father.

I stood up and walked around to another area I wanted to freshen. The squirrel did not run away but only moved closer. I wished the squirrel good morning and continued to feel the completeness of the moment.

About twenty minutes later, I went into the house. I told the squirrel goodbye and thanked him for sharing part of the morning with me. That kind of interaction has never happened again.

*This time it vanished quite slowly,
beginning with the end of the tail,
and ending with the grin,
which remained some time
after the rest of it had gone.*

Lewis Carroll

Chapter 6
Alice's Adventures in Wonderland

Like my father

My Journal

How are you like your loved one?

Visible Blessing –
It's a Wonderful World
April 16, 2006

It had been a year since Mother died and today would have been her ninety-third birthday. I was feeling blue as people do on anniversary dates. Normally Mother's birthday was a cause for celebration.

Years ago my sister and I had begun to associate Mother with Louis Armstrong's song, "It's A Wonderful World." I don't remember Mother talking about the song, but we felt it fit her life, her energy, her spirit. We had wanted it sung at her memorial mass, but the priest apparently felt it wasn't traditional and would not allow it.

And as I said before, I was feeling pretty blue this day. At my lunch break I decided to go to Chico's to distract myself, since shopping is usually fun. While I was walking around I began talking to my mother telling her it was a difficult day and I really needed to hear from her.

Exactly at that moment, "It's A Wonderful World" began to play. I don't know whether the music was coming from the store itself or from somewhere else in the mall. It didn't matter.

At that moment I knew it truly was a wonderful day.

*So don't be frightened, dear friend,
if a sadness confronts you larger
than any you have ever known,
casting its shadow over all you do.
You must think that something
is happening within you,
and remember that life
has not forgotten you;
it holds you in its hand
and will not let you fall.
Why would you want to exclude
from your life any uneasiness,
any pain, any depression,
since you don't know what work
they are accomplishing within you?*

Rainer Maria Rilke

Letters to a Young Poet

Today would have been her ninety-third birthday

My Journal

What anniversaries may be difficult for you? How can you celebrate them, honoring your loved one and lifting your spirits?

Visible Blessing— Mother Bombie
January 15, 2007

When my niece was born, she began calling my mother Bombie. No one knew what it meant but Bombie she was and Bombie she stayed. Through the years, people would ask, "How's your mother, how's Bombie?"

Mother was always a huge *Jeopardy* fan. Anyone who knew Mother well knew 6:00 P.M. was not a good time to call to chat. My husband and I also enjoy *Jeopardy* but following Mother's death we hadn't been watching it for many months. Slowly we begin to restore our regular routine.

One day we were watching the show. I was looking at a photo my sister had just sent, a picture of Mother fishing in her hip boots and waders.

I'll never forget what happened next. The Jeopardy question was, "What is Mother Bombie?"

"Mike," I said, shocked, "did you hear that?" I searched "Mother Bombie" on Google and laughed to myself as I heard Mother telling me for years to look things up and here I was, researching Mother Bombie. Come to find out, *Mother Bombie* was a comedy written by John Lyly and published in 1594.

Who would have guessed there was a correlation?

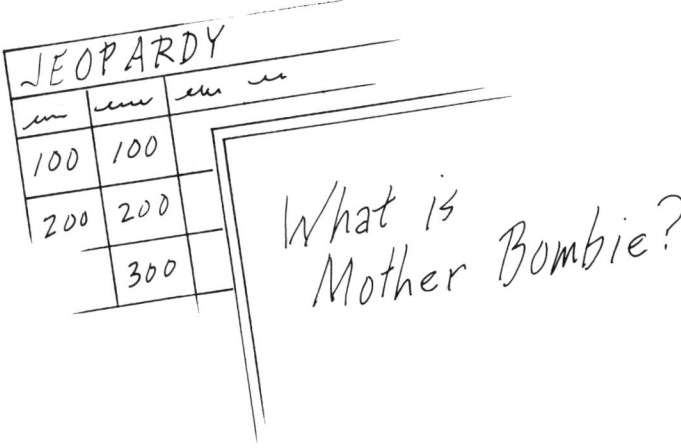

***Coincidence is god's [sic]
way of remaining anonymous.***

Albert Einstein

The World As I See It

Anyone who knew
Mother well knew...

My Journal

What did you know well about your loved one?

Visible Blessing – Pennies
February 5, 2007

I had noticed that Mother often communicated by leaving me a penny. In order to make sure there was an actual communication, I would clear all potential penny sites at the beginning of the day.

As well as an office in Helena, I had a business office in Missoula, the town where Mother lived. I maintained the office for seventeen years, initially going to Missoula weekly and eventually going every other week.

When in town, I stayed with a friend and things worked out quite well for many years. However there came a time in which my friend and I had a major disagreement, and I felt I needed to move. I'm not the type of person who loves change— tend to hunker down, find my comfortable place and not budge. Unfortunately, I was being nudged to make a move. I was fairly panicked because I didn't know where I would stay, I didn't know people who had an available room to rent, and staying in a hotel was financially out of the question.

After a very stressful day I contacted a friend who had space to rent and who was more than willing to let me rent a room. By the end of that day I was pretty frazzled.

I left work intending to go to my new "home." I got into the car, and there was a penny on the running board. A wave of relief washed over me. I knew things would be all right.

> ***Why!***
> ***who makes much of a miracle?***
> ***As to me,***
> ***I know of nothing else but miracles.***
>
> Walt Whitman
>
> *Whitman: Leave of Grass, and Selected Prose*

I felt I needed to move

My Journal

What is uncomfortable in your heart?
Where is the Spirit nudging you to move?

Visible Blessing – Damien and Max
March 17, 2007

Mike and I have three dogs: Toby Tabasco, Sierra and Damien. Damien is a blue tick coon hound, what I consider to be a very handsome boy.

He weighs around 100 pounds and is very vocal. When he feels something is worth paying attention to, he barks and howls to his heart's content. Damien is unusual, to say the least.

No one quite knows what makes him tick. Perhaps it's his haunted look and demeanor; perhaps it's his shyness and timidity. No one knows nor, unfortunately, will they ever know.

Mother and Damien never met as she had passed by the time he came into our lives. I think Mother would have been fearful of Damien, not because of his temperament, but because of his large size and her feeling of personal fragility.

I commissioned a local artist to draw a picture of Mother. I had it sitting on a small end-table with the three gnomes, Shadrach, Meshach and Abednego. I liked the little arrangement and was looking at it one morning when Damien came into the room and noticed the new picture. Very much to my surprise, he began to howl and bark and howl and bark, all the while staring at the picture of Mother. I wasn't sure what to do as this was so unexpected, so I removed the picture and Damien quieted down. As I've said, no one knows what makes Damien tick, so I assumed he was having a bad day and continued on with mine.

The next morning, I put the picture back on the table and waited somewhat anxiously to see how Damien would respond. He went outside and all appeared well. But again, once he was back in the house and became aware of Mother's picture, he started to bark and howl. It wasn't an aggressive bark or an angry bark, as if I can distinguish between the two. Rather, it seemed like a "look at this, pay attention," type of bark.

Once again I put Mother's picture away, somewhat frustrated. I put the picture away for a few days, hoping Damien would somehow adjust to whatever was bothering him. Eventually I put the picture back and waited.

    Again Damien seemed in a good space when the day began. Once more when he saw the picture he began to bark and howl. I had absolutely no idea what to do, what he saw, and had no idea of when it would end. I felt both helpless and hopeless.

    I left Mother's picture out of Damien's sight for several days this time. Not to be deterred, I eventually returned the picture to its rightful place on the little end-table. Damien came prancing by, happy as could be, glanced at the table and continued on with his day. I breathed out, hopeful the crisis had passed.

    Damien never again reacted to the picture. I'll never know what he saw or felt, but I do believe Damien had finally met Mother.

***Deep in the Human Unconscious
is a pervasive need
for a logical universe that makes sense.
But the real universe
is always one step beyond logic.***

Frank Herbert

Book 3, The Prophet
Dune

Mother and Damien never met

My Journal

Who would you like to introduce your loved one to?

Visible Blessing – The Pass
April 16, 2007

It was April, and again it was Mother's birthday. I had always tried to make sure her birthday was a big deal. With mother's sister and niece, myself and perhaps some other friends, we would go to dinner at one of our favorite restaurants, returning home to cake and presents.

Here was another birthday, but this one felt hollow, felt empty, as Mother was gone. I had been working at my outreach office. I started the car and was ready for the two-hour drive home. As I drove I came upon fields with newborn calves. One was standing close to its mother, whether for food or security I couldn't tell. Two others were testing their new legs in a chase.

I headed up the hill towards the pass, hoping the roads would be clear and dry as I am somewhat of a chicken driving on snow and ice. As I reached the top of the pass, I looked right and beheld the most magnificent skyscape I had ever seen. The color palette of bronze, red, burgundy, silver, gold, white, all arranged in whirls and flourishes, would have rivaled the skill and mastery of Michelangelo. I pulled over to the scenic turnout, shut off the car, and sat watching in utter amazement and awe. About a half-hour later the portrait began to dissolve until there was nothing.

For a moment I wished I had a camera but I knew this scene would never leave me. I turned on my car and headed home.
Gift given, gift received.

The first peace, which is the most important,
is that which comes within the souls of people
when they realize their relationship,
their oneness with the universe and all its powers,
and when they realize at the center
of the universe dwells the Great Spirit,
and that its center is really everywhere,
it is within each of us.

Nicholas Black Elk

The Sacred Pipe: Black Elk's Account
of the Seven Rites of the Oglala Sioux (1953),
as told to Joseph Epes Brown

Standing close...
Watching in utter amazement and awe

My Journal

As you stand close, what amazes you?

Visible Blessing – Dime – CD Player
June 8, 2007

I woke up knowing I had a presentation to give that day. I felt calm, although there were a few butterflies in my stomach.

I checked the car to make sure there were no hiding places into which Mother could put a penny or some other coin. Satisfied the car was thoroughly clean, I went to get my morning latte and scone.

Our car is a Subaru Outback, both sturdy and reliable. I like the storage space it offers, especially for my many CDs. There is one peculiar storage space, however, up and to the right, a space almost too small to hold a CD but it is not protected from the sun. For this reason I seldom used it, although it was always there as a backup.

After lunch I went to my meeting, and afterward felt pretty good about the presentation. I planned to meet friends for dinner later but in the meantime, I decided to go back to work. I got into the car and there in that quirky little space was a dime.

"Mother," I said, "I don't understand why you left me a dime, as always before you would leave a penny to announce your presence." Was she telling me I had done an unusually good job? Was she telling me she was proud of me?

Obviously, I'll never know but, as usual when I hear from Mother, my heart feels lighter.

Then one day there really was a wolf,
but when the boy shouted they didn't believe.

Aesop

"The Boy Who Cried Wolf"

In that quirky little space

My Journal

In what quirky little spaces in your life
does your loved one announce their presence?

Visible Blessing – Shadrach, Meshach, and Abednego
March 21, 2008

Mother discovered an artist/sculptor named Dr. Tom Clark. He was world-renowned for his skill and artistry. At one point he created a wood spirit or gnome for himself. Hundreds more were to follow.

Each gnome that he sculpted was unique and magical. Each gnome had its own history. Each was drawn from an actual historical figure, popularly known person, or whatever struck Dr. Clark's incredible imagination.

When Mother came upon the gnomes, she, like so many others, fell in love. Looking through a catalog one day she was particularly drawn to a group of three gnomes named Shadrach, Meshach and Abednego. The names of the three gnomes are found in the book of Daniel, and the three Jewish gentlemen are known for their love of and devotion to God.

The three little gnomes stood 4 to 5 inches high. They were dressed in tunics, some had beards of varying lengths, and one had a walking staff. All looked as though they had wandered through many lands. Each had a small coin hidden somewhere within its sculpture. What was most incredible about the gnomes, however, was the exquisitely detailed work that had been done to make their faces come alive, with twinkling eyes and mirthful grins.

Oh, how Mother enjoyed the gnomes. She placed them on a small end-table facing one another as they stood within a circle. Mother placed them that way so they could have their usual daily conversations.

After Mother died the gnomes came to live with me. I commissioned a local artist to do a picture of Mother in one of her favorite fishing spots. And, of course, I placed her picture within the circle of the gnomes.

One day I was arranging the gnomes, and greeting them along with Mother. The television was on in the room, tuned to *The Price Is Right*. I was half paying attention when I heard someone mention Shadrach, Meshach, and Abednego. I was shocked to hear the names because of the obscurity of the figures. I have no idea who mentioned their names nor do I know in what context the names were mentioned. I looked at Mother, Shadrach, Meshach, and Abednego. And as I looked at them, Shadrach stepped forward and gave me a wink and nod.

***Understanding
means throwing away
your knowledge.***

Thich Nhat Hanh

Being Peace

Each gnome had its own history

My Journal

What is you and your loved one's history?

Visible Blessing – Gibson Park
April 2, 2009

One day I went to Mother's and saw she had purchased two pictures, one a summer scene of Gibson Lake in Montana. There was also a companion piece, a winter scene of skaters on the frozen lake. The pictures were quite different from the type of artwork Mother was usually attracted to. When I mentioned this, Mother said the lake was the spot where my father had proposed. I never thought of Mother as a romantic or as overly sentimental, but I had been wrong.

Mother had gone to a local art dealer and asked them to find or re-create the lake scenes. Those pictures must have brought a feeling of contentment, of continuity between past and present.

I realized that as much as I thought I knew Mother, there was a space she held apart, held private. I wondered what she felt when she looked at her special pictures. Did she recall joyful days? Did she feel nostalgia for what had been?

When Mother passed the pictures came to me. I held them close because having those pictures meant having the younger part of Mother.

One day I was in the kitchen making dinner. The television was on and the newscaster said the birds had returned to Gibson Park. I went into the living room to look at Mother's pictures. "Are you close by?" I wondered. "Is Dad with you?" The pictures were silent and I knew the cycle had been completed.

*That is happiness:
to be dissolved
into something
complete and great.*

Willa Cather

Book 1, Chapter 2
My Ántonia

The Lake was the spot where my father had proposed

My Journal

What is a special place for you and your loved one?
What does it mean to you?

Visible Blessing – Don Juan
May 16, 2009

It was a delicious Saturday morning, the kind of day to do nothing. Everything having to do with my business was finished. And, for now at least, the flower beds were pristine with bold bright buds popping out everywhere.

Normally on a day like this, I would be talking to my mother about everything and nothing. I wandered into my office and looked at the hundreds of books on the shelves. Should I read one of the new books I bought with eager anticipation, and yet left standing on the shelf unopened? Or should I reread one of my favorites, hoping to glean some new insights?

I reached up and my hand touched Carlos Castañeda's *The Teachings of Don Juan.* I wondered whether Mother was close by, and opened at random a page in the book. When I opened the book, the page I turned to said, "It was April 16," which is mother's birthday.

As I read further, Don Juan talked about his use of mortars and pestles to create various concoctions. I smiled. As a pharmacist, Mother often spoke of mortars and pestles. In fact, she had quite a large group of unique and lovely mortars and pestles that she had collected over many years.

I knew Mother was there with me. I've been impressed by the clever ways Mother has found to communicate with me. It seems she is able to use and master the tools of her new environment.

*How often have I said to you
that when you have eliminated the impossible,
whatever remains, however improbable,
must be the truth?*

Arthur Conan Doyle

Chapter 6
The Sign of Four

Talking to my mother
about everything and nothing

My Journal

What past or present conversations linger in your heart?

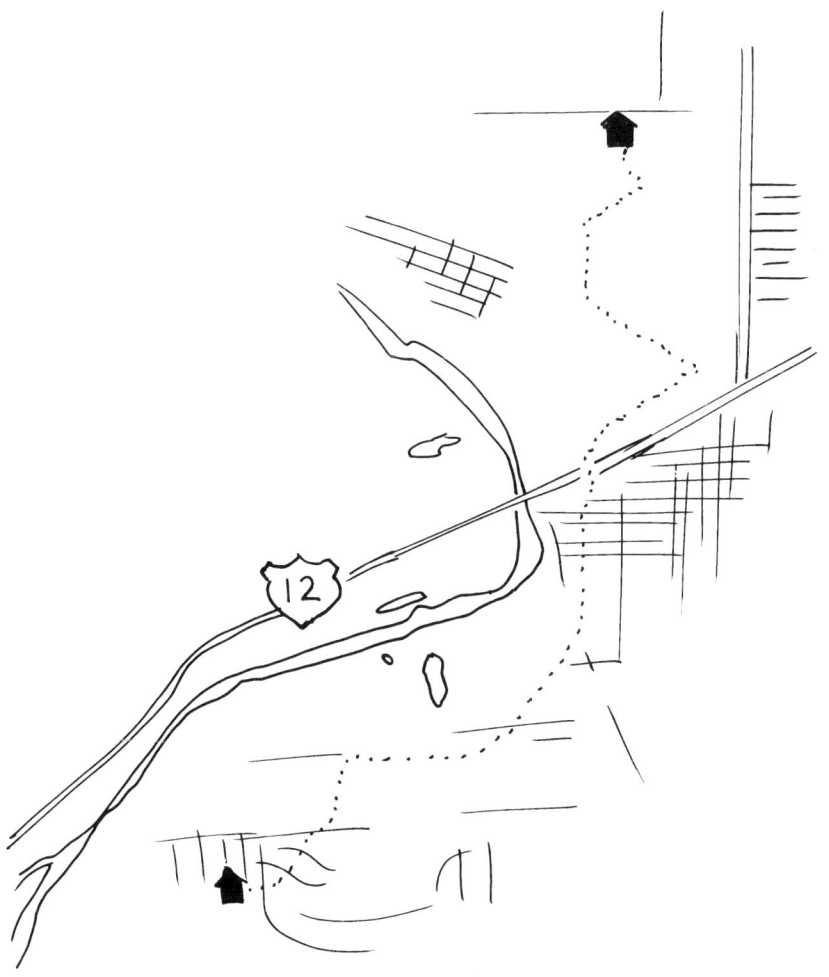

Visible Blessing – Wandering Woman
June 25, 2009

My cousin had just returned home from running some errands. When she pulled into the driveway, she noticed a woman sitting on her front step. The woman appeared to be in her late seventies. When my cousin went to the woman and introduced herself, she realized the woman was somewhat confused. She was trying to reach her son and luckily she had his number.

Vicky called the son, who was frantic because his mother, newly arrived in town, had wandered away from the nursing home where she was now residing. After speaking with the son, my cousin agreed to drive the woman back to the nursing home.

On the way to the nursing home, Vicky learned the woman had grown up in the small Montana town of Oilmont. Ironically Oilmont had been named by my grandfather. When asked, the woman said her father had been employed by my grandfather, and she knew the family well. The woman had gone to school with my aunt in a one-room schoolhouse and she knew my mother. Obviously both my cousin and I were extremely excited by this contact, although we were not clear what the meaning could be.

What was astonishing about this contact was the route the woman took in order to reach my cousin's home. It was not a matter of walking in a straight line for a number of blocks. Rather, the woman had to navigate crossing a major freeway. Several blocks later she crossed the railroad tracks and eventually changed direction to walk uphill an additional eight blocks to arrive at Vicky's house. All of this walking was done in a busy urban area. Even someone familiar with the town would have found the circuitous path to my cousin's home confusing. And yet, it appeared the woman had a destination to reach, a message to deliver.

My cousin and I knew the woman's meanderings were purposeful. We also knew both our mothers had joined together in sending this communication. But why, we wondered. A day later we had our answer.

There was a medical crisis in the family, and my aunt and mother wanted to warn us. We were still a team as we had always been and nothing seen or unseen could dissolve that relationship.

Look at your hand and ask yourself,
"Since when has my hand been around?"
If I look deeply into my hand
I can see it has been around for a long time,
more than three hundred thousand years.
I see many generations of ancestors in there,
not just in the past, but in the present moment, still alive.
I am only the continuation.

Thich Nhat Hanh

"The Sun My Heart"
Thich Nhat Hanh: Essential Writings
Edited by Robert Ellsberg

A message to deliver

My Journal

What message has your loved one delivered?
What message are you called to deliver?

Visible Blessing – Angel on the Tree
December 15, 2009

When Mother moved into independent living in a retirement community, I tried to make her holidays special. I knew they would never be like the days when my father was alive and the family was together, but at Christmas I tried to make things as festive as I could. I would decorate the nature sculpture outside Mother's door with little ornaments and brightly colored balls and bells.

One year I found a shop that specialized in natural plants and they also had an extensive array of decorated artificial Christmas trees. I found one that stood 5 feet high, 5 feet wide. It had an abundance of twinkle lights and golden bows. It was both bright and richly elegant. Some years before Mother and I had gone Christmas shopping and found a delightful little angel, simple yet charming, and the little angel fit perfectly atop Mother's new Christmas tree.

After Mother died, the little Christmas tree came to my home. Every year I would decorate Mother's nature sculpture and bring in the little Christmas tree topped with the angel.

One year, all the boxes holding Christmas decorations were brought into the house from storage. I love Christmas and, joyfully, Mike and I began to decorate the house. I put the bells and balls on the nature sculpture outside our front door and brought in the little tree. I plugged it in and the twinkle lights came alive. I went to get the little angel but the box that held the angel was empty. I began going through other boxes, but none held the angel.

I called Mike and asked him to look for the angel but despite our combined efforts, we could find no angel. I felt the beginnings of panic but remembered to breathe and tried to quiet. I continued checking the remaining boxes, checking the tree itself to make sure the angel wasn't hiding somewhere among the branches. Nothing. I was feeling powerless but thought it was best to let it go and begin anew the next day. I didn't sleep well and was up quite early the next morning. After much of that day was spent looking for the nonexistent angel, we had

no choice but to give up. I didn't let go lightly, but there was no other alternative.

Toward the end of the day, I looked at Mother's little tree and there was the angel right on top where she was supposed to be. Since my husband and I have no children, only three large dogs, and no friends had dropped by that day, we had no idea what had happened. All I knew for sure was that everything was in place; everything was in order at last.

And the little angel stood atop the tree in the midst of the twinkle lights and looked down upon us all.

*I realized it for the first time in my life:
there is nothing but mystery in the world,
how it hides behind the fabric of our poor, browbeat days,
shining brightly, and we don't even know it.*

Sue Monk Kidd

The Secret Life of Bees

A delightful little angel,
simple yet charming

My Journal

Where did you find your little angel of a loved one?

Visible Blessing – Chickadees on the Rail
June 9, 2010

I had just entered my newly redecorated office. I looked around taking in the new hardwood floor, the delicately textured wallpaper, and the newly placed artwork that made the room special.

There was an Italian tapestry with scenes of a bistro with a lake adjacent to the street. An oil painting of a turtle, one we had purchased in Hawaii, was opposite the tapestry. Another wall held an original painting with randomly placed branches, five large colorful leaves, and one small bird peeking out. Mother had loved that picture, and placing it in my office gave a sense of completeness to the room.

I sat in my new rocking chair below Mother's painting of the branches and bird. The door was open, it was summertime, and I looked out the screen door. About 15 feet from my office door was our neighbor's home. Directly outside my office door was a very large lilac bush. The bush was covered with hundreds of beautiful white flowers. The fragrance, almost overwhelming, spoke of the newness of spring.

In all the years of looking out my office door, I noticed that smaller birds like wrens, sparrows and chickadees had never flown into that space, preferring the backyard with the bigger trees and feeders.

Robins loved the lilac bush and had built a nest the year before. I watched the young robins, open mouths waiting for mama to bring a big juicy worm. Several years later the magpies built a nest in the same tree and brought new life once more.

As I looked through the screen door, I was shocked to see eight chickadees marching up and down the railing. I had never seen any birds on the railing, much less Mother's chickadees. Periodically they would fly into the air, only to return to the railing, their antics reminding me of trampoline artists.

"I need to tell Mike," I thought, but realized any movement would disrupt the show.

"Mother, look," I thought. But of course, she already had.

Be grateful for whoever comes,
Because each has been sent
as a guide from beyond.

Jalal al-Din Muhammad Rumi

"The Guest House"
The Essential Rumi
Translation by Coleman Barks

A sense of completeness

My Journal

What momentous items give you a sense of completeness?
Where have you placed them?

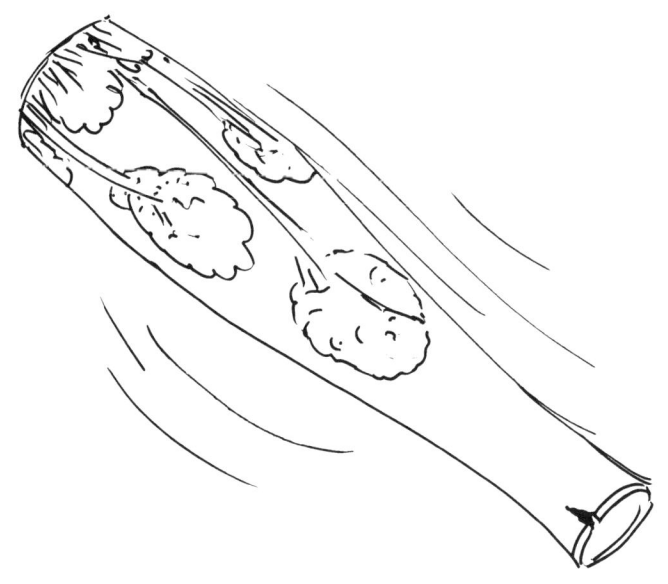

Visible Blessing – The Vase
June 27, 2010

Mother would often volunteer at the Bargain Basement, a thrift store at the church she attended. She and the other volunteers would sort the new items that arrived, getting them ready for display. One day a beautiful English vase was one of the new items. Mother purchased the item and it quickly became one of her favorites.

The vase stands about 17 inches tall and 3 inches wide by 3 inches deep. It is delicately painted in light browns and creams, depicting a summer scene with trees and shrubs. Mother took great care in its placement in her home, trying to ensure its safety. She had the vase for many years. When Mike and I finished the basement in our home, Mother gave me the beautiful vase as a gift. I was both honored by the gift and protective of it.

Mother had passed by this time and as I went downstairs one day, I found to my horror that the shelf had fallen and the vase was on the floor. It had fallen over three feet and was lying on its side. I walked over to it with leaden feet, fearing what I would find. Not only was the vase potentially shattered, but I felt I had been careless with Mother's gift.

When I arrived at the vase it looked unharmed. I gingerly picked it up, and was shocked to find it did not disintegrate in my hands. I found only one small chip gone, about the size of half a kernel of unpopped corn. Of the 25 shelves Mike had meticulously installed, the one with the lightest amount of weight was the one that had fallen. I'll never understand how the vase survived the fall from the shelf. Was Mother somehow involved in cushioning the fall?

As I thought about the vase throughout the years, I wondered what message was being sent. Was it that no matter how much we try to protect and defend ourselves and our loved ones, life has its own plans for us? Was it that we are so much stronger than we know? Or was it that no matter how small or large our fears, we are protected?

I beg you,
to have patience with everything
unresolved in your heart
and to try to love the questions themselves
as if they were locked rooms
or books written in a very foreign language.
Don't search for the answers,
which could not be given to you now,
because you would not be able to live them.
And the point is to live everything.
Live the questions now.
Perhaps then, someday far in the future,
you will gradually, without even noticing it,
live your way into the answer.

Rainer Maria Rilke

Letter 8
Letters to a Young Poet

Trying to ensure its safety

My Journal

Where are you fragile? What makes you strong?

Visible Blessing – Monarch Butterfly
June 28, 2010

My father spent the last years of his life in a nursing home due to ill health. When he passed, the caregivers at the nursing home gave us a colorful paper butterfly. I think it was intended to represent the monarch butterfly. From that day forward, I associated the monarch with my father.

Our home is surrounded by flowers, sides, back, and front. We have hundreds of varieties and, to my mind, it seemed as though it should have been a butterfly haven. Sadly, the butterflies didn't agree with me, and few came even though I had planted bushes that were supposedly surefire butterfly attractors.

One summer day I was outside on the porch. The birds were singing. There was a warm breeze. The dogs were exploring, and all was well. I began talking to my father, telling him how I wished he had been able to visit our home when he was alive. I also told him I could use a little help with our rosebushes, as somehow his skill with roses had not passed on to me.

I looked out at the back yard and to my utter amazement; here came a monarch butterfly, resplendent in its bright yellow and black markings. For a moment I thought of asking if it was in the wrong yard. But then I thought of my father and knew it was right where it was supposed to be. It appeared to explore the yard, touching down lightly on the ponds, landing on many of our flower species, apparently to see if they were satisfactory. Then the monarch flew towards me. Oh, how I tried to encourage it my way, but it appeared to have its own flight plan, as it flew around and around, appearing to miss nothing that it found interesting. It flew over the fence and out of the yard.

"Oh no," I thought, "it's way too soon for you to go." Magically, it seemed to hear and returned to the yard for a few more dainty dives and flourishes. But this was not to last and soon the monarch was gone for good, never returning since that day.

"Lovely, absolutely lovely. Was that you, Dad?" I said. Somehow I felt the warmth of his large hand on my knee, as he said, "Yes, Honey, it was."

Once upon a time,
I, Chuang Chou,
dreamt I was a butterfly,
fluttering hither and thither,
to all intents and purposes a butterfly.
I was conscious
only of my happiness as a butterfly,
unaware that I was Chou.
Soon I awaked, and there I was,
veritably myself again.
Now I do not know
whether I was then a man
dreaming I was a butterfly,
or whether I am now a butterfly,
dreaming I am a man.

by Zhuangzi

As translated by Lin Yutang

I associated the monarch
with my father.

My Journal

What do you associate with your loved one?

Visible Blessing – Dove on the Rail
August 31, 2010

Mother had always been fascinated by birds. Whether she was sitting on the back porch at our family home or out camping in the summer time, a pair of binoculars was always close at hand. So many times she would be drawn deeper into the forest by an unfamiliar bird song she wanted to identify.

When my husband and I moved to a new town, we similarly began to make friends with the many birds that frequented our backyard. It's funny how you don't notice something that's absent until it appears.

One day there was an unfamiliar bird song.

"That's a mourning dove," said Mike. There on the power line was a pair of doves, singing their hearts out. Every season the female would depart to the huge fir tree across the alley where she would build her nest.

One Sunday summer morning I was in my office, slowly rocking, reading a little, dozing a little. The door was open, and through the screen door I could see the robins and magpies in the lilac bush just outside the door. A few moments later, I looked up, and there was the dove on the railing, ten feet away from me.

"What you doing here?" I wondered. "You are usually in the backyard." By this time Mother had passed, and I was used to communications from her. "Did Mother send you?" "Did Dad send you?" I could feel my body revving up. Part of me said, "Take a breath, begin again." I looked at the dove and simply said, "Welcome."

The dove seemed to understand. He settled himself on the railing and began his serenade, "hoo, hoo-hoo." "What do you see," I wondered, "when you look at me?" As I looked at the dove I tried to see beyond bird or dove, looking at the essence of the sturdy little being before me.

"Mother, look," I thought. "What a blessing."

I continued to rock and listen, utterly mesmerized. But then the dove fluffed his feathers, gave me a little bow and flew away. I looked at the clock — it had been fifteen minutes.

I felt a terrible loss as I looked at the now-empty space where the dove had been. As I focused on my breath, I slowly understood. The dove was not "gone" just because I couldn't see him. He had simply moved to another location. As I listened intently, from far away came the familiar, "hoo, hoo-hoo; hoo, hoo-hoo; hoo, hoo-hoo."

*Invisible before birth are all beings
and after death invisible again.
They are seen between two unseens.
Why in this truth find sorrow?*

The Mahabharata in the Bhagavad Gita

textual translations by J. Mascaro
Chapter 2, v. 28

*The dove was not "gone"
just because I couldn't see him.*

My Journal

How is your loved one with you?

Visible Blessing – Solitaire
January 13, 2012

When I bought a new computer I was captivated, unfortunately, by the many fun and intriguing computer games. I settled into a morning routine of coffee, a few games of bridge and my favorite, Free Cell. I knew they were a waste of time, but I comforted myself thinking I was probably staving off Alzheimer's by keeping my brain active.

One day I decided I needed to step out of my rut. I typed "solitaire card games" into the computer's search window. I eagerly clicked the mouse waiting to see what wonderful new games would appear; to my amazement, up popped Maxine's obituary.

My cousin Vicky had given Mother a used computer when Mother was in her late eighties, and although mother never went on-line, she knew how to send and receive e-mail. The fact that the computer connected her to the outside world was all she asked. Mornings would find her, coffee in hand, sending out her greetings.

The more I thought about the file that had just shown up, the more I realized this was Mother's way of saying "Good morning." Although Mother had always maintained she was computer illiterate, I was impressed she had somehow been able to go into the workings of the computer and send me a greeting. As I read the obituary, I was impressed by the extent to which Mother had not only used her talents but had extended and expanded them as well. As I continued my day, I felt a completeness and contentment I had not felt in a long, long time.

111

If you would indeed behold the spirit of death,
open your heart wide unto the body of life.
For life and death are one,
even as the river and the sea are one.

Kahlil Gibran

The Prophet

I needed to step out of my rut.

My Journal

What little thing can you change to reach out to your loved one?

Visible Blessing – Mother as a Young Girl
February 18, 2012

I was thinking of spring and summer flowers. I was looking for one of my favorites, the campanula. I had visions of the beautiful flower in mind as I typed "campanula" into the search screen of my computer. I clicked the mouse and waited. Instead of the flower I had expected to see, I found myself looking at a picture of my mother, age seventeen.

This was the second time the computer had sent me files. To look at the files individually didn't convey the same message as when I looked at them collectively. I realized that the files represented a composite of my mother's life.

As a young woman of seventeen she was vibrant, with a passion for life and many gifts to be developed in her own distinctive style. Her obituary showed a woman of ninety-two at the end of her life. It detailed the incredible journey her spirit had taken through those many years. No matter what Mother faced in her lifetime, she did it with both grace and grit.

Mother, it was a life lived exquisitely.

Growth [is] the only evidence of life.

Newman's summary of a doctrine of the Thomas Scott,

in *Apologia pro Vita Sua: History of My Religious Opinions*

The beautiful flower

My Journal

What were the most beautiful flower moments for your loved one?

Visible Blessing - Milkshake
May 30, 2012

I had just been diagnosed with leukemia and was spending my first day in the hospital. I was both terrified of what was to come and excited at the newness of it all. Friends came and helped me forget for a while. Anxiously I watched as they left, one by one, knowing that soon I would be alone with my thoughts. It was hardest when my husband left, but he had a two-hour drive to return home and I knew he had to go. And then I was alone.

I looked at the dinner menu and saw something that looked fairly good, topping it off with some vanilla ice cream, my favorite.

When Mother was in the retirement community in independent living, we would often get burgers and milkshakes. I know this was not nutritionally the best lunch, but it was fun and we enjoyed the treat. Mother always ordered a chocolate milkshake and I preferred vanilla. My father also preferred a chocolate milkshake, and when I would visit him at the nursing home I made sure I had a chocolate shake in my hand.

That night in the hospital, I finished my dinner and had my scoop of vanilla ice cream. At last it was time to face the solitude and the fear. At that moment, there was a knock on the door and someone from food service came in. "Here's your milkshake," he said brightly.

"I didn't order a milkshake," I said.

"Well, someone in this room did," he said. I took a sip of the milkshake. Of course it was chocolate. I'll never know who sent the milkshake, whether it was Mother or Dad. Actually, I think it's more fun to think that they did it together.

At that moment, I knew I was not alone.

"How does one become a butterfly?"
she asked pensively.

"You must want to fly so much that you
are willing to give up being a caterpillar."

"You mean to die" asked Yellow,
remembering the three who fell out of the sky.

"Yes and No," he answered.
"What **looks** *like you will die*
but what's **really** *you will still live.*
Life is changed, not taken away.
Isn't that different from those who die
without ever becoming butterflies?"

Trina Paulus

Hope for the Flowers

At that moment,
I knew I was not alone.

My Journal

When have you known you were not alone?

Visible Blessing — Cricket Outside
September 16, 2012

We had just arrived in Salt Lake City where I was to receive a bone marrow transplant for leukemia. I had come with all kinds of stories cluttering my mind. Some of the stories said the treatment would be easy, while some of the stories said that the treatment would be incredibly difficult. I just knew that I was absolutely terrified. Hopeful, yet terrified.

"Mother," I thought, "where are you? I need you now."

My husband and I found a nice motel where I would spend the last night before entering the hospital. After we ate dinner I watched as the hands of the clock moved slowly ahead, both a good thing in that it was delaying my entry into the hospital, and yet a difficult thing in that I had more time to worry. I realized there was no going back.

I became aware of a sound both insistent and loud right outside of our window. It was a cricket, making his presence known. Having spent a large part of my lifetime camping in the woods with my family listening to the sounds of crickets, I had no doubt who sent the cricket to me. He sang until dawn.

I loved the cricket song; I felt grounded and comforted, both qualities attributed to the cricket. Glancing often at the clock, I cannot say I slept well that night. But some part of me truly believed I would receive the extremely good fortune the cricket assured me of.

Soon it was morning and, just like the cricket, I prepared to jump into the difficulties ahead.

Without thinking,
the dragonfly darted down.
Suddenly he hit the surface
of the water and bounced away.
Now that he was a dragonfly,
he could no longer go into the water.

"I can't return," he said in dismay.
"At least I tried, but I can't keep my promise.
Even if I could go back,
not one of the water bugs
would know me in my new body.
I guess I'll just have to wait
until they become dragonflies too.
Then they'll understand what happened to me,
and where I went."

Doris Stickney

Water Bugs and Dragonflies

I felt grounded and comforted

My Journal

What strengths help you jump into your difficulties?

Visible Blessing – Doves, Salt Lake City
April 27, 2013

After I completed chemotherapy and received the bone marrow transplant in Salt Lake City, Mike and I rented an apartment so I could continue to be evaluated at the hospital. Every week I would go to the clinic where they drew blood and we anxiously waited for the results. I imagine the doctors and other healthcare professionals wished I could have been less anxious and fearful, but I felt as though I were hanging on by a very slim thread.

Week after week, I went through this routine. Would the numbers be up, indicating healing, or would they be down, indicating trouble? At one point I was told there was an abnormality. The transplant had taken only partially and I was now part donor, part me. I hoped the part that was me was a healthy part and not the one that had been the cancer carrier.

Mike spent his days working remotely, exercising and filling time. Because of a condition known as graft-versus-host disease that could be activated by the sun, I didn't go outside unless I was totally covered. I don't know what I did during those months. Some reading, some walking in the apartment, some meditating, some praying. The days passed by, the weeks passed by, the months passed by.

At long last, six months later, we were released to go home. Although part of me was excited and happy, the clinic had become a source of security, and leaving was both wonderful and frightening.

Of course, I talked to Mother when we were getting ready to leave. "Please let me know," I said, "that things will be all right."

Mike loaded our possessions into the car, and before I knew it, he had the door open, saying it was time to go. I put on my protective sun hat and walked out the door.

To my utter amazement, directly overhead and down the pathway to the car was a flock of eight brilliant doves, white and strong, showing me the path. Rather than flying through the entire courtyard, a very large courtyard, they huddled about me. I climbed in the car, waved good-bye to the doves and we headed home.

The path continues.

***As surely as there is a voyage away,
there is a journey home.***

Jack Kornfield

*After the Ecstasy, the Laundry:
How the Heart Grows Wise on the Spiritual Path*

showing me the path

My Journal

Where is your loved one's path leading you?

Visible Blessing - Sirius Radio
April 27, 2013

Despite the wonderful sendoff by the doves, mile after mile my mind returned to worry-thoughts. To ward off these thoughts, I turned to Mother. "Will it really be okay?" I silently asked her.

When I was growing up, practically from the day I was born, Mother would carry me into my parents' bedroom, sit down in her rocking chair, and sing me to sleep.

How I loved her many songs: "After Dark," "Sleep, Kentucky Babe," "Oh, I Love a Marianna" and, my favorite, "Ragtime Cowboy Joe." I think I particularly liked that song because of its upbeat tempo and jazzy syncopation. By the time I was two or three, I could sing those songs right along with my parents. I can still hear my father's lovely tenor voice, my mother's strong alto voice singing in harmony around a campfire with friends and family.

On our ride home, we tuned the satellite radio to an easy listening jazz channel. I settled in, thoroughly enjoying the music. I watched as the miles ticked by, leading us home. Just then, filtering through the radio we heard "Ragtime Cowboy Joe." Tears sprang to my eyes as I loudly and clearly sang out every word of the lyrics captured in my heart for over sixty years. I reached over to Mike and squeezed his arm. "It's all good," he said.

The world is incomprehensible.
We won't ever understand it;
we won't ever unravel its secrets.
Thus we must treat the world as it is: a sheer mystery.

Carlos Castañeda

A Separate Reality: Further Conversations with Don Juan

"It's all good," he said.

My Journal

What goodness makes you want to sing in thanksgiving to your loved one?

Visible Blessing – Oprah
March 16, 2014

We were finally home and life had returned to normal. Despite my initial apprehension, the dogs were absolutely delighted to see us.

We continued making the drive to my hometown for weekly blood draws to make sure my numbers were headed in the right direction which, thank God, they were.

Then one day I noticed the vision in my right eye was changing. I've lived with multiple sclerosis for forty-three years, so I was somewhat used to strange things happening visually. Slowly, very slowly, the vision worsened in one eye. I became concerned only when I began losing vision in the other eye, as that was very atypical.

I consulted a doctor and he began to monitor my vision. When my vision continued to worsen, he feared I would completely lose my sight in both eyes. He sent me back to Salt Lake City, this time to the Moran Eye Center at the University of Utah. The specialist I consulted presented me with a diagnosis, actually quite an ugly one.

We returned home and I began treatment for the visual distortion. At this time Mike and I were still driving to my hometown once a week for the blood draw and additionally were driving to another town for an eye treatment called aphaeresis. We all thought it was going well, or at least hoped it was, until we got a call from the Moran Eye Center saying I did not, in fact, have the dreaded disease. I was happy, especially because I thought it was a typical flare-up of MS, and I knew all of my flare-ups had eventually gone into remission and healed almost completely.

However, my world had grown smaller. My drivers license had lapsed, I could not read, I could not cook without risking chopping off a few fingers. My husband faithfully took over the majority of household chores.

I had always been a person who had goals and plans, yet now with so many limitations my mood continued to spiral downward. Luckily, during my chemotherapy treatments, I had begun writing a book about the dogs in my life. The book was called *Deb and Her Pups; Stories of*

Loving and Healing. The book kept my mind occupied some of the time.

On a particularly dark day emotionally, I called to my mother, telling her of my fears, my anxieties, my despair.

"I need to grow — I need to learn," I cried out. "I'm terribly afraid I have lost my way."

The morning after I told Mother of my distress, I turned on the television and noticed there was a program recorded on an unfamiliar channel. I was cleaning up the digital video recorder, deleting those programs I no longer wanted. When I came to the unfamiliar recording, my finger was on the delete button when a voice said, "Check it out."

Up popped Oprah Winfrey's "Super Soul Sunday," a program that offers listeners information from healers and teachers of tremendous diversity. Rather than feeling lost or trapped in my present situation, I'd found a door that had suddenly sprung open.

I was reacquainted with some of my favorite guides, such as Thich Nhat Hanh and Ram Dass, and introduced to other ones like Elizabeth Lesser and Eben Alexander, along with many more. My life was once more vibrant and flowing. I had successfully navigated the rapids I had feared would pull me under.

My vision is slowly returning. My hopes are high. I still have no idea where my path will lead.

I am where I need to be. I walk with my guides and helpers who are leading me to my next adventures.

"What makes the desert beautiful,"
says the little prince,
"is that somewhere it hides a well."

The Little Prince

Antoine de Saint-Exupery

*I'm terribly afraid
I have lost my way.*

My Journal

In what ways can you mentor others as your loved one guided you?

Visible Blessing – "Ragtime Cowboy Joe"
May 17, 2014

It was May. The sky was a crystalline blue, the songbirds were back in full force, and we even had a flicker gracing our yard. I turned to Mike and asked, "Do you think mother will be okay with the book being published?"

"I think she'll be just fine with that," Mike said. And with that he was off to the grocery store to buy orange juice for breakfast.

I continued to ponder, hoping he was right and mother would in fact be pleased with the book.

Soon Mike was home with a grin on his face. "They had three guys at the store playing banjos and guitars, doing a Kingston Trio kind of act." These local performers only come once or twice a year.

"Sounds fun," I said. "What were they playing?" Mike turned to me, eyes twinkling, "Ragtime Cowboy Joe."

139

*"**We are** not *separate.*
We are inextricably inter-related."

Thich Nhat Hanh

Thich Nhat Hanh: Essential Writings
"Roses and Garbage"
Edited by Robert Ellsberg

The sky was a crystalline blue

My Journal

What will make the mystical sky in your life crystalline blue?

Afterword
July 12, 2014

Since these past years of fire, when my old life and old ways were burned away, I'm slowly learning to let go more easily, trust more deeply. I remember to take a moment and let go of the distracters, turn off the noisemakers and step outside. I listen to the nature symphony that surrounds me: the buzzing of the bees, the rustling of the leaves, the distinctive melodies of the summer song birds. I look at the blue of the sky, knowing that as day turns to night like a curtain, the blue of the sky will be drawn back to reveal billions of dancing, twinkling stars with worlds yet to be explored. I feel this mysterious place around me. I am this sacred space.

Don't say that I will depart tomorrow —
even today I am still arriving.
Look deeply: every second I am arriving
to be a bud on a spring branch,
to be a tiny bird, with still-fragile wings,
learning to sing in my new nest,
to be caterpillar in the heart of a flower,
to be a jewel hiding itself in a stone....
Please call me by my true names,
so I can wake up
and the door of my heart
could be left open, the door of compassion.

Thich Nhat Hanh

"Please Call Me by My True Names"
Thich Nhat Hanh: Essential Writings
Ed. by Robert Ellsberg

Deborah Nelles, MA, MSW, Licensed Clinical Social Worker, Licensed Addiction Counselor, Certified in EMDR, Retired
was born and raised in Missoula, Montana. A graduate of the University of Montana, she desired to study and heal others, which led to a master of arts in sociology from McMaster University in Hamilton, Ontario, Canada, followed by another MA in social work from Eastern Washington University in Cheney.

Deb now lives in Helena, Montana with her husband Mike and their beloved three dogs, Toby Tabasco, Sierra, and Damien.

Linda McCray, MFA, CSD is a visual artist, spiritual director and teacher. Beginning her day with sacred readings and a sketchbook, art as meditation, has drawn her into a deeper relationship with her Creator. She illustrated Deb's story and wrote reflection questions to welcome you to journal your story by drawing and/or writing. Linda also creates abstract spiritual original paintings and art-and-faith retreats. She is a Sister of Charity of Leavenworth Associate, and an adjunct art professor for Helena College University of Montana, University of Mary, and Loyola University Chicago.

A Flock of Doves Publishing, LLC
We are working on our next book with after they're gone experiences from readers. If you would like to share your story, please submit it through our website, AFlockOfDoves.com.

Deb and Her Pups by Deborah Nelles will be published soon.

Books are available on amazon.com and at your local book store.